HEARTLAND HEALTHCARE SERVICE'S
PROBLEMATICAL ERROR AND ALTERNATIVE SOLUTION

A Project Presented to the
Faculty of Spring Arbor University

in partial fulfillment of the requirements
for the degree of Bachelor of Arts

by

Nikki Giovanni Barnett

Paula Lipper

MOD T-55

May 25, 2010

Certification Page

This is to certify that the Project Thesis prepared

By: Nikki Giovanni A. J. Barnett

Entitled: Heartland Healthcare Service's Problematic Error and Alternative Solution

Has been accepted by the faculty of Spring Arbor University.

_____
Academic Coordinator

This Project Thesis is to be regarded as confidential and its use as a sample in future classes is restricted.

_____
Site Contact

Table of Contents

ABSTRACT 4
CHAPTER ONE: DESCRIPTION OF THE PROBLEM 7
STATEMENT OF THE PURPOSE 7
SETTING OF THE PROBLEM 7
SIGNIFICANCE OF THE PROJECT 13
CONCLUSION 13
CHAPTER TWO: LITERATURE REVIEW 14
CONTROLLED SUBSTANCE PROCESS 14
CONTROLLED SUBSTANCES AND PHARMACIES 17
CONTROL SUBSTANCES AT HHS AND LTC NURSING FACILITIES 20
REFERENCES 26
CHAPTER THREE: OPTION SELECTION 28
CHAPTER FOUR: DESCRIPTION OF THE PROPOSED INTERVENTION 32
DATA COLLECTION PLAN 33
DATA ANALYSIS PLAN 35
CONCLUSION 36
CHAPTER FIVE: THE EVALUATION PLAN 37
ANALYSIS DESIGN OBJECTIVE ONE 37
ANALYSIS DESIGN OBJECTIVE TWO 38
ANALYSIS DESIGN OBJECTIVE THREE 38
DATA ANALYSIS PLAN 39
LIMITATIONS OF THE DATA COLLECTION PLAN 40
CONCLUSION 41
CHAPTER SIX: SUMMARY OF RESULTS 47
CHAPTER SEVEN CONCLUSIONS & RECOMMENDATIONS 57
APPENDIX A: REFLECTIONS 65
DEFINITION OF TERMS 73

Abstract

The purpose of this project is to choose a problem that one would like to solve thoroughly by research, designing a specific plan of action and writing an extended report. This project thesis is about the implementation and evaluation of the controlled substance process within Heartland Healthcare Service's (HHS), which is a pharmacy that supplies medications to long term care facilities.

There are two key elements involved in this problematical error. The first element is the dispensing methods of the level II controlled substances to the facilities and clients. The other key element is the communication process between the physician, facilities and HHS that consist of receiving a signed order for level II controlled substances from the physician immediately to dispense a regular day supply of the CII to our facilities for their patients.

The DEA's overall goal is to eliminate the current dispensing system and have Omnicare Corporations implement a new process for legal purposes that meet the regulations of the CSA. The difficult task is being able to implement a new process at HHS while being able to maintain current production flow. Due to the system fit error a lot of revenue has been lost as the end results of many fines, therefore HHS cannot afford to do a company shut down during the implementation.

There are three objectives involved in the alternative solution to fix the system fit error. The first objective is to send controlled substances at a level III-V in place of the level II controlled substances from HHS to the facilities until level II medication that was originally ordered is available for shipment. A ninety-five percent acceptability rate on turnaround time is necessary as well as a pain relief percentage of at least fifty percent, with seventy five percent also given to customer satisfaction.

Objective two consist of the order entry process changing from one order type for medication entry to another order type to decrease the turnaround times of delivery. HHS will no longer use an RXP profile only order type to enter level II-V medications and in its place a send only RX order type will be used for entry. This is to decrease the turnaround time from HHS to the facilities by at least fifty percent. The expected increase needs to have a significant percentage of at least eighty-five for timely arrival of the medication from the pharmacy to the facilities.

Objective three involves positive results of more satisfied than discontented long term care facilities if they receive CIII-V medications in place of CII medications until the CII's are available for shipment. Facility satisfaction includes medication arrival time, pain relief and patient satisfaction. When involving customer satisfaction overall a satisfaction rate should be at least seventy-five percent leaving twenty-five percent for errors.

The data analysis and research design was produced using the percent and chi-square method. Chi squared can be calculated by adding up all of the conducted surveys for evaluation from objective one through three, and breaking them down based upon a one-hundred percent scale of time, efficiency and satisfaction. This helped determine whether or not the new implementation process would be a success. Alternatives were given as last resort options if the resolution to the system fit error was unsuccessful. The alternatives did not have a positive overview for the future of HHS. It consisted of alternatives such as branch closings, elimination of positions, pay cuts for all employees, and possible mergers with others branches.

Finalizing all research and concluding the project thesis, the positive outcome of the resolution to the system fit error has been implemented within HHS and other branches of the pharmacy as well. This project thesis will discuss the resolution to the system fit error, the restructuring of the controlled substance process; the use of proper skill and technique that was involved during the data analysis and statistical methodology. This project thesis alternative solution will not only meet the requirements of the DEA, but first and foremost it will eliminate the problematical error altogether at Heartland Healthcare Services.

HHS's Problematic Error and Alternative Solution

Chapter One

Description of the Problem

Introduction

The purpose of this project is to choose a problem that one would like to solve thoroughly by research, designing a specific plan of action and writing an extended report. This project thesis is about the implementation and evaluation of the controlled substance process within Heartland Healthcare Services (HHS), which is a pharmacy that supplies medications to long term care facilities.

Statement of the Purpose

The purpose of this project is to design, implement and evaluate the controlled substance process enabling pharmaceutical providers the ability to provide emergency supplies of controlled substance medications to long term care facilities in timely and accurate manner, and thus remaining within the boundaries of the regulatory protocol set forth by the Drug Enforcement Administration, the Food and Drug Administration and the Controlled Substance Act.

Setting of the Problem

The scope or extent of pharmacy practice entails more conservative roles such as compounding and dispensing medications. Services that are more modernly related to patient care involve clinical services, reviewing medications for safety and efficiency and providing drug information. There is a variety of areas where a pharmacy can exist including but not limited to; retail, hospitals, clinics, nursing homes, drug industries and regulatory agencies, and with every different location comes many guidelines for operation.

Omnicare is the leading provider of pharmaceutical care for seniors. Omnicare is a pharmaceutical company that provides services for millions of residents of skilled nursing, assisted living, and other healthcare facilities in 47 states and Canada. While doing the mentioned, Omnicare captures an immense amount of data, combines this data with its patented problem solving procedures while utilizing their advanced technologies. This procedure is based upon the best practices in geriatric medicine to identify and help treat diseases in the elderly.

Omnicare also oversees the structure and functions of Heartland Healthcare Services (HHS), which is known as a sub division of the Omnicare Corporation. Heartland Healthcare Services is also inter-grouped with other organizations such as HCR Manor Care and Arden Courts.

Heartland Healthcare Services consist of approximately 500 employees. There are six branches in total with limitless organizational boundaries. These branches vary in location and are as follows: Allentown, Sunrise, Woodridge, Largo, Arden Courts and Toledo more frequently known as HHS and the HUB, central station where Pharmacy Services and Order Entry handle all of the actual orders. The other branches check, package and ship the medications only. The other five branches have approximately one hundred to three hundred employees.

Each branch has many departments with size varying at each individual branch, and each being unique in playing their part for helping dispense medications to our customers with an exceptional ETA's, estimated time of arrival. The various departments include: Pharmacy Services, Customer Care and Order Entry, Clinical Intervention, Point of Sales (Billing), Accounts Receivable, Warehouse, Delivery Drivers, Maintenance, Intravenous Medications (IV Dept.), Scanning, Packaging, Inventory, Control Substances, Intake, Human Resources, Payroll, Benefits, Corporate Compliance, Medical Records, IT, Quality Assurance, "The Cage" (Locked cage of employees handling and processing CII and CIII, controlled substance prescriptions with a level II and possible III classification) and the Pharmacists (RpH) have their own department as well.

As part of an Omnicare Corporation, Heartland Healthcare resides under a formal functional structure with rules, procedures and written documentations such as manuals and job descriptions that commend the rights and duties of the employees. HHS operates as a twenty-four, around the clock pharmacy; maintaining three well-staffed shifts which provide above average turnaround times and accuracy of medications to their clients. The clients consist of Long Term Care (LTC), Supported Living (SLF), Assisted Living (ALF) and Hospice facilities. HHS is centralized with most decisions made at the top or executive level therefore; HHS also operates as a mechanistic organizational system. HHS is also very resource dependent being that they rely on pharmaceutical manufacturers to supply their medications. When involving complexity, HHS actually lies within both environmentally stable and complex with few integrating roles, minimal boundary spanning, and an extensive planning process with forecasting and high-speed responses.

Each department within HHS has a regional manager and three supervisors that report to the managers for all three shifts, where tasks are broken down into specialized separate parts. Every shift has lead technicians or team leads that report to the supervisors. The individual managers report to the vice presidents and of course, Vice presidents report to the CEO and President of our organization. Between The President and the CEO are the attributes of the Corporate Compliance Officers. They play a major part of handling issues with the FDA, Food and Drug Administration and the DEA, Drug Enforcement Administration. That entails the brief summation of the power structure and task environment of HHS.

    The corporate culture of HHS is extremely adaptive. There are many opportunities for advancement and it is based upon values, beliefs and thoughts meaning if one puts forth themselves as a top-level employee, he or she can become part of the management team. The decisions are based upon but not limited to one's professionalism. Other key factors include background, attendance, acquired skills, knowledge of pharmacology, certifications, a two to four year degree in a Science or Health Information related field, accuracy of a task being 95% or above and being able to process a minimum of sixty medications an hour. This is a standard protocol regardless of your department excluding Scanning, Packaging, Clinical Intervention and Intravenous Medications. These are critical key factors and necessary for upper management positions and a successful career at HHS. If one lacks in any of the said areas, one must be able to account for the difference by having another skill or becoming cross-trained to be a more valuable asset to the company as a whole.

    HHS also has many incentives and bonuses for meeting specific and crucial deadlines, supplying medications to new facilities, meeting quotas in various departments, having few or no work related injuries and successful launches of new software. They also acknowledge birthdays, employee anniversary dates, holiday bonuses, company picnics, company outings and warehouse sells on excessive or outdated office supplies. HHS also takes part in many organizational events such as Walk for Wishes, Breast Cancer Awareness, "Penny Wars"; which supports our troops, The United Way (includes incentives for donating) and many more, HHS also has a weight watchers group that entails HHS battling other branches for the most successful amount of weight lost overall.

      The technology used to process our medications entered within HHS from start to finish is driven with our Oasis Software System as our primary source of technology for holding data. A server known as an Esker Software Server is the source of technology that allows us to view document images. Regardless of the department, one can view everything needed for standard protocol and a task or assignment can be completed using this software. It is considered user friendly once one can grasp the concept of the function keys needed to achieve the standard protocol. Basic training is required and typically consists of a two to three week training period depending on the individual's computer knowledge.

      The overall power and political aspect of HHS resides within the hands of the FDA, Food and Drug Administration and the DEA, Drug Enforcement Administration whom work directly with our Corporate Compliance Department. HHS just as any other pharmacy has to follow all of their guidelines with every order processed from over the counter medications to controlled substances. The FDA and the DEA sets the standards for what is acceptable and unacceptable for the pharmacy. The CEO, President, Vice President and Corporate Compliance Officers then pass on their request and demands to the managers, supervisors and employees. Without a say in the matter HHS either abides, or becomes a target for massive audits and prolonged investigations.

History and Background of the Problem

There are two key elements involved in this problematical error. The first element being the dispensing methods of the level II controlled substances to the facilities and clients. This entails the emergency dispensing or short supply method until a regular supply can be issued to the facilities. This must be done in a timely matter and a sufficient quantity or supply must be sent to meet the needs of the patients. The other key element is the communication process between the physician, facilities and HHS that consist of receiving a signed order for level II controlled substances from the physician immediately to dispense a regular day supply of the CII to our facilities for their patients.

The DEA's overall goal is to eliminate the current dispensing system and have Omnicare Corporations implement a new process for legal purposes that meet the regulations of the CSA. Therefore, to avoid losing any of the branches or to eliminate possible mergers HHS has to devise a time sensitive solution to halt fines and eliminate revenue loss overall, due to this problematical error.

The resolution involves restructuring the controlled substance process; and with the proper skill and technique, HHS should and will be able to eliminate this issue while managing to process old prescriptions as well as new. A limitative boundary issue is trying to find a strategic plan that can work around and eventually fit into the current workflow with the least amount of errors; thus continuing the current production flow as well.

Significance of the Project

The importance of this project is that if all HHS departments involved follow the provided design, implementation and evaluation process as presented, HHS would not only meet the requirements of the DEA, but also eliminate the problematical error altogether. The resolution to the problematical error would demonstrate an exceptional example of a company, HHS amongst other Omnicare organizations being committed to doing so to maintain excellence and integrity within their corporation. The solution to the error deems as straightforward and very effective if all involved department managers take the time and implement the resolution to their staff accurately and precisely.

Conclusion

In the conclusion, this chapter presented the purpose of the project and included a discussion regarding the setting and the goal pointing out the scope and limits of the problem. Which the goal being to have all of the departments at Heartland Healthcare Services work together to eliminate the problematical controlled substance dispensing error by communicating as a structured team while utilizing the designed intervention process. A definition of terms has also been included and will help identify many terms in chapter two. Chapter two consist of a literary review of the controlled substance process overall, the controlled substance process within pharmacies and the controlled substance process involving servicing long term care (LTC) nursing facilities.

Chapter Two

Literature Review

Introduction

This chapter is for the purpose of providing published literature related to the controlled substance process under three different branches. The branches include the controlled substance process overall, the controlled substance process within pharmacies and the controlled substance process involving servicing long term care (LTC) nursing facilities. This chapter will provide a broader view of the controlled substance process while revealing differences among the different settings, thus bringing forth new ideas, evaluating outcomes and alternative solutions.

Controlled Substance Process

The FDA or the USFDA is an agency of the United States Department of Health and Human Services and is responsible for controlling the sale and use of drugs, including the licensing of new drugs for human use (Johns, 2002). The FDA is also responsible for regulating and supervising the safety of foods, dietary supplements, drugs, vaccines, biological medical products, blood products, medical devices, radiation-emitting devices, veterinary products, and cosmetics. The FDA enforces section 361 of the Public Health Service Act and the associated regulations, including sanitation requirements on interstate travel as well as specific rules for control of disease on products. (U.S Department of Health & Human Services, 2007)

The DEA is the lead agency for domestic enforcement of the drug policy of the United States and implemented the CSA, Control Substance Act of 1970, which is the federal U.S. drug policy under which the manufacture, importation, possession, use, and distribution of certain substances is regulated. Known as a System for U.S. compliance with international treaties, the CSA is the legal foundation of the Federal government's authority over controlled substances and listed chemicals. The CSA has consolidated over 50 laws regulating the manufacture, distribution, import, export and dispensing of controlled substances and listed chemicals. The Act also served as the national implementing legislation for the Single Convention on Narcotic Drugs (USFDA, 2009).

The legislation created five schedules or classifications, with changeable qualifications for a substance to be included in each. Two federal agencies, the DEA and the FDA determine which substances are added or removed from the various schedules, though the statute passed by Congress created the initial listing. The American Pharmacists Association (2007) states that classification decisions are required to be made on criteria; including potential for abuse and currently accepted medical use in treatment in the United States. This also applies to international treaties. The DEA does not define or regulate medical practice standards. There are no federal laws or regulations that put limits on the quantity of controlled substances that may be prescribed. Some states or insurance providers may limit the quantities of controlled substances prescribed or dispensed (USFDA, 2009).

Schedule I through V have distinctive characteristics of each class. Schedule I medications have a high potential for abuse and consist of drugs that have no current acceptable medical use in the United States (Cocaine). Schedule II medications have a high potential for abuse and the drug or other substance has accepted medical use in treatment in the United States or a currently accepted medical use with severe restrictions (Percocet & Dilaudid). Schedule III medications drugs or other substances that have a potential for abuse less than the drugs or other substances in schedules I and II and abuse of the drug or other substance may lead to moderate or low physical dependence or high psychological dependence (Tylenol 3). Schedule IV medications are drugs or other substances that have a low potential for abuse relative to the drugs or other substances in schedule III and abuse of the drug or other substance may lead to limited physical dependence or psychological dependence relative to the drugs or other substances in schedule III (Xanax). Lastly, Schedule V medications are for medical purposes only and drugs or other substances that have a low potential for abuse relative to the drugs or other substances in schedule IV and abuse of the drug or other substance may lead to limited physical dependence or psychological dependence relative to the drugs or other substances in schedule IV (Phenergan & Codeine Syrup) (Cornell University, 2009).

Although not classified under the controlled substances but still related for legality measures is medical marijuana. A pharmaceutical product, Marinol, is widely available through prescription. It comes in the form of a pill and is also being studied by researchers for suitability via other delivery methods, such as an inhaler or patch. The active ingredient of Marinol is synthetic THC also know as Tetrahydrocannabinol or Dronabinol, which is the main psychoactive substance found in the Cannabis plant (INCB, 2009). This has been found to relieve the nausea and vomiting associated with chemotherapy for cancer patients and to assist with loss of appetite with AIDS patients. There are no FDA-approved medications that are smoked. Smoking is generally a poor way to deliver medicine. Unlike smoked marijuana, which contains more than 400 different chemicals, including most of the hazardous chemicals found in tobacco smoke,

Marinol has been studied and approved by the medical community and the Food and Drug Administration (DEA, 2009).

Controlled Substances and Pharmacies

A prescription drug can be defined as one that has been ordered or prescribed by a physician or other licensed prescriber to treat patients (American Pharmacists Association, 2007). In order to be legal, a prescription must be issued by a registered practitioner, for a legitimate medical purpose and in the usual course of professional practice (USFDA, 2009).

Practitioners are not limited in their ability to prescribe, administer, or dispense narcotics to persons with intractable pain. The corresponding responsibility rests with the pharmacist who fills the prescription. Within a pharmacy there are specific labels that must be present on any container when dispensing controlled substances. This is known as the controlled substance mark, it is on levels (CII-CV). This mark indicates the control category of a drug with a potential for abuse.

Manufacturers must clearly label controlled drugs with their control classification. Distributors are required to maintain accurate records of controlled substance activity. This includes accurate records of inventory and drugs dispensed. Schedule II narcotics must be kept for seven years and all others must be kept for two, unless state requirement is different. Schedule II prescriptions must be kept separate from non-controlled drug records in the pharmacy, though in some cases they may be kept with other controlled drug records (American Pharmacists Association, 2007).

By law within a pharmacy both the prescriber and the dispenser of the prescription have joint responsibility for the legitimate medical purpose of the prescription. This is to assure the controlled substance is being prescribed for appropriate reasons thus deeming the purpose of a DEA number. All prescribers of controlled substances must be authorized by the DEA. They are assigned a DEA number which must be used on all controlled drug prescriptions. Controlled substances have greater requirements at both the federal and state levels than other prescriptions. Schedule II drugs must have the DEA number on the prescription and the patients name and full address must be present in order to dispense from the pharmacy.

On schedule II prescriptions the form must be signed by the provider. In many states there are specific time limits that require Schedule II prescriptions to be filled promptly. Quantities are limited and refills are not allowed. Federal requirements for Schedule II-V are less stringent than schedule II. Faxed prescriptions are allowed and they may be refilled up to five times within a six month period. Although some state regulations may be stricter than the federal requirements. One must be aware of the requirements within their own individual pharmacy.

Besides the DEA, CSA, FDA and the State board of Pharmacy there are various professional bodies and associations which set and maintain pharmacy standards for dispensing controlled substances as well as regular medications. The American Society of Health-Systems Pharmacists (ASHP) is an accrediting organization for pharmacy residency and pharmacy technician training programs. They **represent pharmacists who practice in hospitals, health maintenance organizations, long-term care facilities, home care, and other components of health care systems** (ASHP, 2009).

The United States Pharmacopeia (USP) is a voluntary not for profit organization that set standards for the manufacturer and the distributor of drug and related products in the United States. The standards are referred to by federal and state laws and are published in the United States Pharmacopeia and the National Formulary. The USP Drug Product Problem Reporting (DPPR) program has worked toward identifying and improving defective and potentially unsafe drug products for over thirty years. This organization conducts a lot of experiments involving various uses of controlled substances (USP, 2009).

The Joint Commission on Accreditation of Health Care Organizations (JCAHO) is a non-profit organization that established and monitors compliance. JCAHO evaluates health care organizations and inspires them to excel in providing safe and effective care of the highest quality and value (JCAHO, 2009). These services are provided to healthcare programs in the United States such as hospitals, healthcare networks, health maintenance organizations (HMO) and nursing facilities.

The American Society for Consultant Pharmacists (ASCP) sets standards of practice for pharmacists who provide medication distribution and consultant services to nursing homes. It is organizations such as the ASHP, USP, JCAHO and ASCP that make the controlled substance process primarily more complicated when dispensing and delivery is involved to nursing facilities from pharmacies. The reason is there are already vigorous amounts of guidelines, protocols, rules and restrictions from the DEA, CSA and FDA, in addition to standards from the individual accrediting organization. This in turn leaves minimal room for successful dispensing and basically non-existent room for errors when the pharmacy is dispensing controlled substances to nursing facilities. Another issue for nursing facilities is a lot of medications are for comfort care so controlled substances need to be dispensed twenty four hours a day, seven days a week, furthermore creating communication issues with the facility because they are unaware of exactly how many steps are needed to dispense Schedule II-V medications, while continuing to uphold DEA, CSA and FDA standards.

Control Substances at HHS and LTC Nursing Facilities

Over the past year the DEA has audited four pharmacies and has made necessary adjustments for interpretations and guidelines to the control substance policy when providing Schedule drugs to long term care patients in nursing facilities. Three major industry changes have been made that affect HHS and Long Term Care (LTC) Facilities.

The first major change stated that the physician nurse relationship is not valid in Long Term Care facilities for controlled substances. The DEA states that a nurse employed by the nursing home is not an agent of the physician and cannot order controlled substances for patients from pharmacies by simply writing it down and faxing it to the pharmacy. However the doctor can request the nurse to be an agent for this particular medication, dosage and refill numbers. The nurse must then call the pharmacy and give the order verbally to the pharmacy as well as the faxing of the chart order. Both must be done to comply with the law (DEA, 2009).

The second major change that involves the distribution of medications from HHS to the LTC is the emergency dispensing of medication from the emergency box, which is a locked box of schedule drugs that is located with the long term care facility is valid only for new medication orders on patients only after the other options are exhausted including CIII to CV medications. CII medications cannot be removed from the emergency box, which is a box located within nursing facilities for easy access to medications without a verbal approval from the physician and pharmacy. Refill medications for existing patients and residents are not considered and emergency just because it was not ordered or sent from the pharmacy. There is no flexibility to these rules (Collaborative Pharmacy, 2009).

The last major change states that all controlled substances must have the patients' name, address, city, state and zip code on each prescription. The DEA has decided that nursing homes are considered as retail prescriptions similar to CVS, Walgreens and Kroger's. In hospitals, the DEA has allowed the nurse to be an agent of the doctor and thus is able to order any medications that the doctor orders for the patient with complying by retail rule (DEA, 2009).

HHS is trying their best to comply with all of the new implementations being set forth by the various agencies and they are also actually creating many handouts with new rules and regulations for the processing and shipment of their orders. One of the main documents currently being used until HHS can validate and implement a new controlled substance process is a handout on the overview of the Order Entry/PV1 (Prescription & Verification Stage One) unsigned controlled substance prescriptions at a level II. This handout explains what is meant by partial fills, recommended quantities, what the pharmacists are to do with the unsigned requested orders, where the order is to currently sit and or wait until approval has been granted, this being done by receiving a signature from the attending or house physician and information on whether or not the allowance of dispensing the medication to the facility is mentioned in one of the main handouts that is being utilized as basically a guide for the controlled substance order entry process. (Heartland Healthcare Services, 2009 *Handout*)

Within HHS the Controlled Substance department, the managers and lead technicians are struggling through the new rules and regulations trying to cope and accommodate to the best of their abilities, at the same time while receiving demands from the DEA and FDA, HHS has to in turn set out demands for controlled substance technicians which basically is not alleviating any of the stress at this point. The work flow has been documented in the C2 handbook and is as follows: Every one hour someone needs to fax out the NR's (No Refills) that are created and need signatures. The pharmacists will have to call and get a verbal emergency supply if HHS cannot obtain a signed script for the day on these particular scripts. The C2 technicians must try to assist the pharmacist in obtaining signatures. When the scripts come back signed it is priority to scan them in because the scripts will go out to retrieve signatures scanned depending on how they were entered. If at all any quantities or direction change on the script it must be re-routed to the Order Entry department to be cancelled off the patient profile and re-entered (Heartland Healthcare Services, 2009 *Handout*)

Due to the new implementation process from the DEA and FDA including the CSA involving all controlled substances at a level II currently requiring a signature before being released to facilities, HHS has now enforced a previously used controlled substance process which is known as the Dr. Letter Tracking Files System. This system actually involves the "how to" process on the upkeep of prescriptions and signatures when working with so many different branches, pharmacies, physicians and patients. Due to the purpose of this thesis and how the current implementation process will flow, the consideration to keep the Dr. Letter Tracking Files is at a high probability due to the nature of the files linking into the resolution to the system fit error. (Heartland Healthcare Services, 2009 *Handout*)

A major part of the implementation process for the project thesis involves HHS using what is known as Tickle Files (TIC). Tickle files is simply a filing cabinet located behind the C2 technicians that holds extra prescriptions. If for some reason the doctor ends up signing more than one script for the same drug, HHS will dispense off of one of the scripts and put the other in the Tickle File for future use. HHS only enters a script as a TIC if the C2 technicians write it on the signed prescription. It is basically being entered into the computer as a TIC order type so when the last of the current supply is depleted, HHS order entry technicians can see that there is another script waiting to be dispensed without getting another doctors signature. This process would deem fit to stay in place and help with the structuring of the proposed implementation and or alternatives to the controlled substance process helping alleviate the system fit error. (Heartland Healthcare Services, 2009 *Handout*)

This briefing basically states that HHS as well as other pharmacies that service LTC nursing facilities must fax all prescription order forms to the doctor's office for Schedule CII through CV medications. The problem with this statement is that it is indeed set in stone for level CII medications but as for now HHS and assuming other suppliers to LTC nursing facilities have leniency with level CIII-CV medications. It is important that each order is received in a timely manner from the facility. Once either the primary care provider or attending physician signed or provided verbal authorization and the nurse's fax is received, the medications can then be dispensed to the facilities for the patients. HHS is no longer able to dispense Schedule II medications without this authorization. Due to HHS being a major supplier to LTC's, HHS still has minimal time left from the DEA and the FDA to dispense level CIII-CV medications before a signature is required. The facilities can continue to order refills for medications with refills remaining. (Heartland Healthcare Services, 2009 *Handout*) This is indeed a national event that is taking place between pharmacies that service long term care facilities. All providers of long term care facilities including HHS have and or will be changing the process immediately to comply with the code of federal regulations, while working on a way to completely redesign the structure so the delivery process still meets the needs of the patients and facilities.

After stating some of the necessary guidelines needed at this point for HHS to continue to process level II medications, the need for an alternative and or new implementation process should begin to make more sense and the importance of implementing soon should also be clearer. The mentioned guidelines and handouts utilized by HHS even though helpful all are part of the system fit error, because it compiling work on top of work without being able to deliver and return revenue. With all these steps and processes just to satisfy the DEA, FDA and CSA it is all but impossible to have a decent turnaround time at this point which recaptures the need for the elimination of the system fit error.

Summarizing the three branches of the controlled substance process including the overall view, the controlled substance process within pharmacies and the controlled substance process involving servicing LTC nursing facilities, this chapter presented the literature review by discussing pertinent information for the restructuring of the controlled substance process within Heartland Healthcare Services. Chapter three will entail the positives and negatives of three options and conclude why of the three, option one was chosen as the best fit for the project.

References

American Pharmacists Association (APhA). (2007). *The Pharmacy Technician.* Morton Publishing Company, Englewood, Co

American Pharmacists Association (APhA). (2007). *The Pharmacy Technician Workbook & Certification Review.* Morton Publishing Company, Englewood, Co.

American Society for Consultant Pharmacies, (2009). ASCP. Retrieved August 28, 2009, from ASCP Web site: http://www.ascp.com

American Society of Health-System Pharmacists, (2009). ASHP. Retrieved August 28, 2009, from ASHP Web site: http://www.ashp.org Collaborative Pharmacy. (2009).

Physicians & Clinical Staff for LTC Patients [Brochure]. Miamisburg, OH: Collaborative Pharmacy Cornell University, (2009). Cornell University Law School. Retrieved August 28, 2009, from Cornell University Web site: http://www4.law.cornell.edu/uscode/html/uscode21/usc_sup_01_21_10_13.html

Heartland Healthcare Services. (2009). *Schedule II-V Dispensing Process & Changes* [Brochure]. Toledo, OH: Heartland Healthcare Services.

Heartland Healthcare Services. (2009). *Schedule II-V Dispensing Process & Changes* [Handout]. Toledo, OH: Heartland Healthcare Services.

International Narcotics Control Board, (2009). INCB. Retrieved August 28, 2009, from INCB Web site: www.incb.org

International Narcotics Control Board. (2009). *List of Psychotropic Substances Under International Control* [Brochure]. United Nations Vienna, Austria: INCB.

Johns, Merida L. (2002). Health Information Management Technology: An Applied

    Approach. Chicago, IL: American Health Information Management Association.

Joint Commission on Accreditation of Health Care Organizations, (2009). JCAHO.

    Retrieved August 28, 2009, from JCAHO Web site:

http://www.jointcommission.org

U.S Department of Health & Human Services. (2007). *Health Information Technology*.

    Retrieved from http://www.hhs.gov.

U.S. Drug Enforcement Administration, (2009). DEA. Retrieved August 28, 2009, from

    DEA Web site: http://www.dea.gov

U.S Food & Drug Administration, (2009). USFDA. Retrieved August 28, 2009, from

    USFDA Website: http://www.fda.gov

U.S Pharmacopeia, (2009). USP. Retrieved August 28, 2009, from USP Web site:

    http://www.usp.org

Chapter Three

Option Selection

Introduction

Deciding which option is the best for the purpose of the thesis is determined based on the option and problem connection, or the relationship that brings the two together. There are many techniques involved when making a decision on which option was best suited for the thesis based on the requirements of each option and what was needed for the selected individual topic.

Option One

Option one is the Applied Design Intervention. This option designs a specific intervention to alleviate the problem stated. The intervention must be designed, implemented and evaluated within the time limits of the overall curriculum. This is not a proposal but an active interventional program that will be evaluated in the end to help correct or alleviate the problem.

Option Two

Option two is the Grant Proposal Submission, which is similar to option one except for one major difference. Instead of actually implementing the program during the curriculum, one must submit a proposal to a foundation or agency for funding. The program then will be implemented if the grant is approved.

Option Three

Option three is the Alternative Policy Decision. This option states to submit an alternative policy proposal to a supervisor or board of decision makers evaluating at least three alternatives and their consequent strengths and weaknesses. The individual is to then choose the one that deems best, supporting choices with objectives, hypotheses and relevant data.

Option Selection

Option one was decided for the option selection of the project thesis after reviewing all three options being that the topic of discussion was to implement a new active controlled substance process for Heartland Healthcare Services. Option one was the best fit for the topic discussion and the project thesis due to the fact that it could either help correct or alleviate the problem under the guidelines, rules and regulations of the DEA and the FDA. Option two and three were not the best options due to option two was a grant proposal and HHS is a major pharmacy with specific grant guidelines thus making site contact information limited. Option three was not the best option due to the fact that the restructuring of the control substance process isn't a proposal; it's a requirement from the DEA and FDA. An implementation process is necessary but a policy proposal is not.

Conclusion

After analyzing each option and discussing the options with the site contact at HHS, the conclusion has been made that the amount of availability and or resources, time needed, likely effectiveness of the option and ease of the implementation process were major factors when deciding that option one was indeed the best suited option for the restructuring process of the problem. The fact that the designed specific intervention can be implemented and evaluated within the time limits of the overall curriculum was an important issue as well when deciding which option best relates to the problem. After choosing option one of three as the option for the thesis project, the description of the intervention will be defined briefly but in detail in chapter four.

Chapter Four

Description of the Intervention

Statement of Evaluation Objectives

This chapter entails the nature of the problem in question and the objectives involved for the correction of the problem. Again, the two key elements are the same as previously mentioned. The first element being the dispensing methods of the level II controlled substances to the facilities and clients. This entails dispensing emergency or short supply medications to the facilities until a regular supply can be issued. This must be done in a timely matter and a sufficient quantity must be sent to meet the needs of the patients or residents.

The other key element involved in the summary is the communication process between the physician, facilities and HHS that consist of receiving a signed order for level II controlled substances from the physician immediately to dispense a regular day supply of the CII to HHS facilities for their patients. Both key elements mentioned involve three to possibly four objectives that entail reductions of the errors and increases of the overall satisfaction and controlled substance process at HHS.

Objective One

The first objective is to send controlled substances at a level III-V in place of the level II controlled substances from HHs to the facilities until level II medication that was originally ordered is available for shipment. A ninety-five percent acceptability rate on turnaround time should also be a factor due to the level II-V medications having lower processing standards compared to level II medications. This process will also help relieve pain by at least fifty percent and should provide customer satisfaction of at least seventy-five percent until arrival of the original level II medication is received, which is better than no pain reduction at all especially for terminally ill and or chemotherapy patients.

This objective is to be initiated and fulfilled as soon as possible and is being included due to customer satisfaction being number one within the field of pharmacy. Without customer satisfaction HHS would have no clients, therefore a decrease in revenue.

Objective Two

Objective two consist of the order entry process changing from one order type for medication entry to another order type to decrease the turnaround times of delivery. HHS will no longer use an RXP profile only order type to enter level II-V medications and in its place a send only RX order type will be used for entry for any and all level II-V medications from here on out that are routine and or both routine and as needed with the exception to Duragesic also known as Fentanyl patches due to the dosing being every seventy two hours. This is to decrease the turnaround time from HHS to the facilities by at least fifty percent.

The expected increase needs to have a significant percentage of at least eighty-five for timely arrival of the medication from the pharmacy to the facilities in order for HHS to utilize this order type first and for most from initiation time until the DEA has advised HHS that this process is no longer acceptable, but that is speaking in regards to plan limitations and is not wishful thinking. This objective needs to be initiated and fulfilled as soon as possible just as objective one.

The major change in order types will actually be shown with the higher percentage under the level CIII-V medications, which is indeed the process to eliminate the system fit error. RXP verses RX order type processing for CII medications is actually very similar in time due to the fact that both order types are dealing with level II narcotics. This objective, just as objective one is being included due to customer satisfaction being number one within the pharmacy field and without customer satisfaction we would have no clients therefore revenue would be limited.

Objective Three

Objective three involves positive results of more satisfied than discontented LTC's if they receive CIII-V medications in place of CII medications until the CII's are available for shipment. Satisfaction of medication arrival time, pain relief and customer satisfaction is also necessary. This objective also consists of whether or not facilities are angered by receiving CIII-CV medications in place of CII's until arrival from HHS to LTC's.

When involving customer satisfaction overall a satisfaction rate should be at least seventy-five percent leaving twenty-five percent for errors. Objective one and two are cohesive with objective three; objective one including an expected satisfaction increase of at least eighty-five percent for timely arrival of the medication from the pharmacy to the facilities. Satisfactory arrival time must be no less than ninety-five percent for CIII-V medications and a satisfactory pain relief scale of fifty percent is also expected. The pain relief scale indirectly links to customer satisfaction as well.

Description of the Proposed Intervention

The proposed intervention and resolution involves restructuring the controlled substance process: and with the proper skill and technique, HHS should and will be able to eliminate this issue while managing to process old prescriptions as well as new. A limitative boundary issue is trying to find a strategic plan that can work around and eventually fit into the current workflow with the least amounts of errors; thus continuing the current production flow as well.

When discussing the proposed alternative, HHS would then not only meet the requirements of the DEA, but also eliminate the problematical error altogether. The resolution to the problematical error would demonstrate an exceptional example of a company, HHS amongst other Omnicare organizations being committed to excelling and showing integrity within their corporation. The solution to the error deems as straight forward and is very effective if all involved department managers take the time and implement the resolution to their staff accurately and precisely.

Data Collection Plan

The data collection methodology includes a self developed satisfaction survey that was given to thirty various clients of HHS facilities ranging from Toledo, Ohio to West Palm Beach, Florida. Responses range from strongly agree to strongly disagree with a medium response of neutral. A self-developed timed study survey was created for level II controls versus level III-V controls questioning twenty-eight LTC employees, and a similar self-developed survey for RX versus RXP order types; twenty-eight surveys as well. All of this data helps to determine which the best method for delivery is. It makes for an easy comparison of the old process verses the new alternative solution. Also, this determines which medication of level II –V narcotics will ship faster from HHS to LTC's. All data was obtained from third shift LTC employees.

Lastly, a common questionnaire was created based upon talking with a pharmacists and LTC's. It is more of a self developed question and answer sheet that was created based upon answers to common questions that arise from the LTC's to the pharmacist in regards to level III narcotics. This is titled *"Ask a Pharmacist"* and it is basically an accumulation of frequent questions from LTC's asked to various HHS pharmacists. All data was collected during 9pm and 9am, third shift operating hours. All facts and numbers used for statistics were based upon the mentioned data collection above. All data collected was used in the implementation process of the intervention and change began to take place as more data resulted positive. Due to the immediate need for a resolution to the system fit error, the change took place while data was still being collected, although enough data proved positive for the implementation process to take effect within the first three months of proposing and testing the resolution.

There are many manuals and handouts explaining the controlled substance policy at HHS, which in turn were all used in the implementation process. Currently HHS has roughly five different handouts on how to process level II medications, proper techniques on how to explain to facilities that their medications may be delayed and information containing the procedural change implemented from the DEA involving the CSA. As far as the processing of narcotic orders, there are many order type additions and eliminations involved with the new implementation process. The definition of order type; the pharmacy technicians must specify what type of order they are entering to be processed depending on what the medications is, controlled substances and non controlled substances. These various order types actually become a major factor in the data collection and analysis process.

Some things that help determine the order type are as follows: whether or not the facility needs the medication held or sent, whether or not it is an CII-V med and or narcotic, medications requested for a later dispensing date or just information about the medications for the medical record only, meaning no medications are sent to the facility also known as profile only.

The various order types help determine a client's medication status within the pharmacy. These order types include an NRX order type which is a prescription order type that is not sent and basically a flag for the pharmacy that prior authorization is needed, a regular RX order type which is a prescription order that is sent to the facilities, a PF order type which means profile only and do not send the prescription to the facility, and a RXP which is similar to an RX although the first fill is held instead of sent until the facility is in need of the medication. RX and RXP order types will later be involved in the intervention description and actually become a major factor in eliminating the system fit error. The mentioned order types coincides with the dispensing of the controlled substances at a level III-V temporarily until the original requested narcotic is available.

Data Analysis Plan

The analysis was done using the percent and chi-square method. Basically, adding up all of the survey results and breaking them down into percent categories based upon time, efficiency and satisfaction. This helped determine if the new implementation process was successful or not.

What had become almost certain is that during the implementation process of this current intervention to fix the problematic error, other issues are arising at the same time. So in order to correct one issue other alternatives would have to be put in place as well. The data analysis was performed based upon the most recently released information and guidelines from the DEA. As the year continues the guidelines and criteria continue to change leaving minimal room for one resolution. HHS must continue to add on the proposed intervention and or alternative method while leaving room for errors. The controlled substance process is such a biased area; the following objectives should suffice any and all possible changes given to HHS from the DEA along the guidelines of the CSA. Ideally the implemented alternative solution will be able accommodate the many changes with minimal alterations.

Due to the complexity of the situation being that HHS is dealing with the release of controlled substances a step down from the level I narcotics, which has the highest severity level, all information will be within the electronic computer system as well as the actual hard copies used to keep track of all medications and the current controlled substance process at HHS. Basically the delivery process will enhance for security purposes and with more restrictions as compared to level III-V and non controlled substances.

Conclusion

Concluding the objectives and the description of the intervention, chapter five will discuss the evaluation plan to give a better overview of the data collection, analysis design and plan limitations for the new dispensing method for level II controlled substances. At that point there will be information providing details as to what type of studies are used and what surveys and questionnaires are involved for the actual analysis.

Chapter Five

Evaluation Plan

Introduction

This section will describe the design used for the various types of data analysis involved in this project thesis and the resolution to the system fit error. The name of the research design used, the population involved, location of the obtained data, special precautions and the manner in which the data will be analyzed will be stated during the evaluation plan.

There are many ways that the data for the project thesis can be analyzed but the most beneficial way to analyze the controlled substance process alternative is based on what is known as the percent and chi-squared methods. Using the stated methods for analyzing the studies that have been compiled for the control substance process data will be calculated and results will be given to determine if the resolution to the system fit error has deemed as successful. Details for calculating methods for each objective also known as the evaluation process includes; data collection, data analysis plan. Limitations of the data collection plan are given as well.

Objective Analysis Design Objective One

The first objective analysis design begins with objective one involving the controlled substances at a level III-V. This objective states that level III-V controls will arrive before level II controls when leaving HHS in route to LTC's. The data collection plan for this objective consists of twenty-eight surveys as well with the inclusion of adding CII vs. CIII-V medications. This will also be a timed process from the time the order is received on the pharmacy fax machine all the way to the completed order reaching the facility. This is to determine how long it will take CII medications versus CIII-V medications to reach the pharmacy. Objective one also entails controlled substances at a level III-V taking just as long as level II controls when leaving HHS in route to LTC's. This data collection plan entails using previous data and using twenty-eight total surveys of CII verses CIII-V medications. This will be a timed process from the pharmacy beginning upon the received faxed prescription, ending with the completed filled medication order reaching the long term care facility door. This is to determine how long it will take from beginning to end to process an order.

Objective Analysis Design Objective Two

Objective two involves a prescription order type also known as a RX order types will take just as long as RXP order types to reach the LTC's from HHS. The data collection plan for this analysis will consist of a total of twenty-eight surveys of each RXP and or RX order type. This will be a timed process from the time received on the pharmacy fax machine all the way to the completed order reaching the facility. This is to determine how long the entire process will take. Objective one will also determine whether or not an RX order type will arrive before a RXP order type when leaving HHS going to LTC's.

Objective Analysis Design Objective Three

Objective three involves positive results of more satisfied than discontented LTC's if they receive CIII-V medications in place of CII medications until the CII's are available for shipment. The data collection plan for this objective will consist of thirty total surveys to determine customer satisfaction. This objective also consists of whether or not facilities are angered by receiving CIII-CV medications in place of CII's until arrival from HHS to LTC's. This has been included to determine satisfaction levels.

Data Analysis Plan

The data analysis plan has been created using timed case studies for different controlled substance delivery resolutions and a satisfaction survey that was created to determine the level of satisfaction being received at the facilities. The surveys are illustrated for each objective. The completed surveys will determine the accuracy and satisfaction percents of the implemented resolution to the system fit error on a one hundred percent scale involving the controlled substance process. All data being collected during third shift pharmaceutical operating hours and the data will be given to LTC's that also operate during third shift; operating hours are between 9pm and 9am.

Another analysis plan that was created was an interview between a few individuals in the LTC's. This interview takes place with consulting pharmacists at HHS regarding some common questions and answers (Q & A) to help alleviate some of the stress involved with the controlled substance process changes issued by the DEA and the FDA. The interview entails the top frequent questions that are asked when facilities inquire about the controlled substance process changes and typical responses that they will receive. This was a simple analysis the allowed HHS to create an *"Ask the Pharmacist"* handout to send to all the facilities for a slight ease of mind throughout all of the changes and implementations underway at HHS. The Q & A is also referenced in detail in this project thesis. The (Q & A) "Ask a Pharmacist" handout was created and based upon the implementation process of the resolution to the system fit error.

All of the data for objectives one through three were obtained within HHS and HHS LTC facilities. Due to the fact that HHS operates twenty-four hours a day the data compliment was completed on the third shift clock hours which were actually better than first and second shift due to minimal chaos and interruptions on third shift as opposed to daytime operating hours. The data will be analyzed on a percent scale using the chi-square method with the inclusion of a percent scale determining the significance in the frequency numbers. Using the percent and chi-square method, this consist of adding up all of the survey and or study results and breaking them down into percent categories based upon time, efficiency and satisfaction. This helped determine the success rate of the new implementation process was successful or not.

Special precautions that need to be taken into consideration to remove bias in the data are very vital to the analysis. That is to be sure when analyzing and conducting studies the correct level of controlled substances C-I or II through C-V are being used because if any of the levels are incorrect the data will be incorrect for the entire analysis.

Limitations of the Data Collection Plan

There are a few plan limitations that could exist if the data analysis plan is in effect as previously mentioned. The majority of the data analyzing will be completed between the hours of eleven at night and seven in the morning when third shift analyzing can be completed. Situations could arise if the data results begin to skew negatively in the beginning which would mean no positive results or very limited positive results. Alternative plans of action would be ignoring the rules of the DEA and keep receiving the fines to satisfy the facilities temporarily until we can have a legit and revised plan with seventy-five to one hundred percent positive outcomes. Another option would be to close some of the smaller LTC's to make up for the lost revenue which was and is the base of the initial problematic effects of the system fit error.

Speaking of behalf of plan limitations the DEA has began to talk about not only revising the CII controlled substance process but soon they want to revise the CIII-V controlled substance process to make them all uniform, which would mean the same guidelines would apply for all CII-CV controlled substance medications. Signatures would be required for all of these medications and the use of non-signatures would become nonexistent for CIII-V medications.

If and when the DEA actually pursues this and is at a finalization stage a lot of the data for this project thesis will be irrelevant and the proposed plan of action to fix the system fit error will be null and void due to the fact that a major portion of the process was to eliminate the error by replacing CII's medications temporarily with CIII-V medications. On the other hand the elimination of an order type would still be beneficial because data reveals that one order, the new processing method is indeed faster than another order type, the old processing method. Adjustments would have to be made to the data to possibly determine if it's easier to get signatures for CIII-V versus CII medication. Again, this is just talks of plan limitations.

Conclusion

In summation sending controlled substances at level III-V will provide minimal relief for the pain due to it still not being high enough doses of narcotics as previously sent for terminally ill patients, chemotherapy patients and such, therefore it is going to be a complicated task overall to achieve one hundred percent satisfaction to completely satisfy the requirements requested from the DEA. HHS is trying to accommodate at the highest positive percentage level possible, even though there were limits for calculating data.

Further in detail when moving forward into chapter six; the summary of results for the data analysis will be given to explain in depth the outcomes and effectiveness of the intervention and the evaluation process. Chapter six will also detail what the results of the chi-square and percentage calculations after analyzing. Also included will be the current status of HHS in relation to resolving the system fit error and if the proposed resolution has meant the minimum requested percentages are believed to be successful.

Objective One (RX vs. RXP)

	1-5 Hours	**5-10 Hours**	**10-15 Hours**
Stage Process			
RX Order Type CII's			
Order Entry Process	9	17	2
Order Check & Confirmation Process	25	3	0
Order Shipment Process	28	0	0
Totals	*62*	*20*	*2*
RXP Order Type CII's			
Order Entry Process	13	11	4
Order Check & Confirmation Process	19	4	5
Order Shipment Process	28	0	0
Totals	*60*	*15*	*9*

RX will arrive sooner than RXP and or RX & RXP will arrive at the same time
Accepting and rejecting factors using chi factors and more entailing explanations with charting if necessary
(Twenty-Eight Total Surveys)

Objective Two (CII VS CIII-CV's)

	1-5 Hours	5-10 Hours	10-15 Hours
Stage Process			
CIII-CV Order Type			
Order Entry Process	*27*	*1*	*0*
Order Check & Confirmation Process	*28*	*0*	*0*
Order Shipment Process	*26*	*1*	*1*
Totals	*81*	*2*	*1*
RX Order Type **CII**			
Order Entry Process	9	17	2
Order Check & Confirmation Process	25	3	0
Order Shipment Process	28	0	0
Totals	*62*	*20*	*2*
RXP Order Type **CII**			
Order Entry Process	13	11	4
Order Check & Confirmation Process	19	4	5
Order Shipment Process	28	0	0
Totals	*60*	*15*	*9*

CIII-V MEDS will arrive sooner than CII MEDS and or CII & CIII-V MEDS will arrive at the same time Accepting and rejecting factors using chi factors and more entailing explanations with charting if necessary **(Twenty-Eight Total Surveys)**

Objective Three (SATISFACTION SURVEY)

CIII-CV	SD Strongly Disagree	D Disagree	N Neutral	A Agree	SA Strongly Agree
Questions					
I was satisfied with the time of my medication	4	2	12	10	2
I was able to provide relief using the alternate medication	0	0	2	21	7
I do not mind using the medication until original ordered CII arrives	6	2	9	5	8
I prefer to have the original CII and no alternate CIII-V medication until its available	1	3	6	5	15
The resident is requesting original CII or creating issues regarding CII ordered	9	3	8	5	5
CIII-CV took just as long as would have the CII order	15	9	3	2	1
The physician is not okay with receiving the CIII-V in place of CII until available	2	5	11	7	5
I prefer to continue this process to assure a pain medication for the resident	2	0	3	4	21
I was satisfied with the entire order process	3	1	11	3	12
TOTALS	42	25	65	62	76
Data Analysis	*SD, D, N, A, SA (strongly disagree, disagree, neutral, agree, strongly agree)*				

(30 TOTAL SURVEYS) Nine Question Satisfaction Survey

ASK A PHARMACIST INFORMATION	
(Q) My patient is in pain and need relief ASAP. What can I do to ensure that I am meeting my patient's needs?	(A) When the prescriber calls to discuss the patient's condition encourage the prescriber to write a valid prescription withal required elements and fax the prescription to the pharmacy.
(Q) What elements are required for a valid written prescription for a controlled substance?	(A) Full name and address of the resident, name, strength, and dosage form of the controlled substance medication; number of dosage units or volume to be dispensed; directions for use, name address and DEA number of the prescribing physician; signature of the prescribing physician.
(Q) What if the subscriber does not have immediate access to a fax machine?	(A) Request that the prescriber call the pharmacy or prescribe a non-controlled medication temporarily that does not require a written prescription.
(Q) I have a signed discharged summary from the hospital which has an order for a C-II. Does this authorize me to remove an item from the CS-EDK?	(A) The discharge summary does not constitute a valid written prescription as all of the required elements of a prescription are not usually present.

This Q & A guide was created with the assistance of a consulting HHS pharmacist.

Chapter Six
Summary of Results

Introduction

In this chapter a summation of the results to the evaluation plan in chapter five will be presented using data in table figure. The first thing mentioned in this chapter is what chi-square consists of and how it is broken down to help understands the analysis process. The objective is given and the actual results follow. This breaks down the totals of the percentages needed of the raw data calculated compared to the actual results after all studies and surveys had been completed; data is provided in numerical order from objective one through three. What is taken from this chapter is the positive feedback in relation to system fit error.

Chi-Square Results

Results of the data show significance in the frequency number for all data collected for objective one and two using the Chi-Square method. Since each category was broken down on a time frame it is easier to determine that the results coincide with the new implementation process. There is a actual percent increase with the transition from CII RXP to CII RX and lastly CIII-V RX, which is the key implementation process results being positive also leaving the delivery hours decreasing down to one to five hours. This is the primary success rate for delivery on all medications including CIII-V RX order types with over 100 percent for significance in the frequencies. In further notation, that the new implementation process is succeeding over the previous methods.

Chi-Square and Significance in the Frequency with Percentages

It is concluded that when using the Chi-Square factor if the computed is higher than tabled, there is significance in frequency numbers. Reverse is true if computed is lower. Then interpret. Steps to follow for computation and confidence level outcomes are listed below as well as the results to objective one and two. Objective three results will follow further in this chapter.

Confidence Levels

d.f	99% (.01)	95% (.05)	90% (.10)
3-1=2	9.21	5.99	4.60
5-1=4	13.28	9.49	7.78
d.f. number of categories - 1			

STEPS TO FOLLOW:

1. Actual count for each category
2. Average of categories
3. Subtract average from each frequency
4. Square the difference and divide by the average
5. Add resultant figures
6. Compare answer (computed chi-square value) with tabled chi-square value

Objective One & Two Results CII RX Order Type

Step	1-5 Hours	5-10 Hours	10-15 Hours
1	62	20	2
2	28	28	28
3	62-28 = 34	20-28 = -8	2-28 = -26
4	(34x34) = 1156	(-8x-8) = 64	(-26x-26) = 676
5	1156/28 = 41.29	64/28 = 2.29	676/28 = 24.14
%	**62/84 = 73.8 %**	**20/84 = 23.8 %**	**2/84 = 2.4 %**
6	41.29+2.29+24.14 = 67.72 SIGNIFICANCE IN THE FREQUENCY NUMBERS (d.f. =3-1=2)		

Objective One & Two Results CII RXP Order Type

Step	1-5 Hours	5-10 Hours	10-15 Hours
1	60	15	9
2	28	28	28
3	60-28 = 32	15-28 = -13	9-28 = -19
4	(32X32) =1024	(-13X-13) = 169	(-19X-19) = 361
5	1024/28 = 36.57	169/28 = 6.03	361/28 = 12.9
%	**60/84 = 71.43 %**	**15/84 = 17.86 %**	**9/84= 10.71 %**
6	36.57+6.03+12.9 = 55.50 SIGNIFICANCE IN THE FREQUENCY NUMBERS (d.f. = 3-1 = 2)		

Objective One and Two CIII-V RX Order Type Only

Step	1-5 Hours	5-10 Hours	10-15 Hours
1	81	2	1
2	28	28	28
3	81-28 = 53	2-28 = -26	1-28 = -27
4	(53X53) = 2809	(-26X-26) = 676	(-27X-27) = 729
5	2809/28 = 100.3	676/28 = 24.14	726/28 = 26.0
%	**81/84 = 96.42 %**	**2/84 = 2.4 %**	**1/84 = 1.19 %**
6	100.3+24.14+26.0 = 150.44 SIGNIFICANCE IN THE FREQUENCY NUMBERS (d.f. = 3-1=2)		

Objective One

The first objective was to send controlled substances at a level III-V in place of the level II controlled substances from HHs LTC's until level II medication that were originally ordered are available for shipment. A ninety-five percent acceptability rate on turnaround time was a factor due to the level III-V medications having lower processing standards compared to level II medications. This is due to the fact that as stated previously level III-V medications have lower dependence risk. This process was to help relieve pain by at least fifty percent.

A fifty percent pain relief scale was used due to the fact of also previously stated we have to include delivery of medications to terminal patients as well, and some level III-V will only provide so much relief also including maximum daily doses not to exceed for these alternative levels that are being sent in place of level II narcotics. Again this is still better than no pain reduction at all until the arrival of the level II narcotics, which was the previous process especially for terminally ill and or chemotherapy patients.

Objective One Actual Result

A 95 percent acceptability rate on turnaround time was the expected factor for CIII-V medications. The data shows an actual percent of 96.42. This is compared to a 73.8 percent for turn around with CII RX order types 71.43 percent on turn around for CII RXP order types, thus stating that the new implantation process is 20 percent better in terms of delivery over the old process.

The data also shows a minimal difference between CII RX and CII RXP order types with a percentage difference of 2.37, thus stating that RX and RXP order types for CII medications are very similar in time.

The new implementation process was to help relieve pain by at least 50 percent and should provide customer satisfaction of at least 75 percent as well although customer satisfaction will be mentioned in depth in objective three. Actual survey results show when asked if pain relief was provided using alternate CIII-V medications, the results were 21 of 30 agreeing and 7 of 30 strongly agreeing therefore 28 of 30 surveyed felt that the alternate method provided pain relief leaving a percentage result of 93 percent.

Objective Two

Objective two consist of the order entry process changing from one order type for medication entry to another order type to decrease the turnaround times of delivery. HHS will no longer use an RXP profile only order type to enter level II-V medications and in its place a send only RX order type will be used for entry for any and all level II-V medications from here on out that are routine and or both routine and as needed with the exception to Duragesic also known as Fentanyl patches due to the dosing being every seventy two hours. This is to decrease the turnaround time from HHS to the facilities by at least fifty percent.

The expected increase will be at least eighty-five percent satisfaction for timely arrival of the medication from the pharmacy to the facilities in order for HHS to utilize this order type first and for most from initiation time until the DEA has advised HHS that this process is no longer acceptable, which hopefully will not happen. This objective needs to be initiated and fulfilled as soon as possible just as objective one.

Objective Two Actual Result

Actual results previously show a 73.8 percent for turnaround in one to five hours with CII RX order types and a 71.43 percent on turn around for CII RXP order types, thus stating that the new implementation process is 20 percent greater in terms of delivery over the old process; the new CIII-V process has a percent of 96.42. This is less than 5 percent from 100 percent and an 11 percent advantage over the projected outcome. The major change in order types is actually shown in the table with the higher percentage under the level CIII-V medications RX order type one to five hour return, which is indeed the process to eliminate the system fit error.

The data results listed previously also show RXP verses RX order type processing for CII medications is actually very similar in time due to the fact that both order types are dealing with level II narcotics, thus showing a minimal difference between CII RX and CII RXP order types with a percentage difference of 2.37. This data helps state that RXP order types for CII medications take just as long as RXP order types thus showing the irrelevancy in the need for the RXP order type for dispensing.

In addition to the results above a 75 percent satisfaction rate was necessary for delivery time as well. The data results show 24 of 30 surveyed stated they were satisfied and or neutral with the delivery time which is 80 percent satisfaction on delivery 40 percent each going to agreeing and neutrality. This also coincides with the 96.42 percent delivery of CIII-V medications in one to five hours.

Objective Three

Objective three involves positive results of more satisfied than discontented LTC's if they receive CIII-V medications in place of CII medications until the CII's are available for shipment. This objective also consists of whether or not facilities are angered by receiving CIII-CV medications in place of CII's until arrival from HHS to LTC's. This objective also consists of whether or not facilities are angered by receiving

CIII-CV medications in place of CII's until arrival from HHS to LTC's. This objective involved pain relief satisfaction and overall arrival time satisfaction as well all due to the fact that objective three is about customer satisfaction.

Objective Three Actual Result

When involving customer satisfaction, an overall satisfaction rate should be at least 75 percent leaving 25 percent room for errors. The arrival times should still have a percent of 95 for satisfaction for CIII-V medications and a 50 percent satisfaction for pain relief from the previous objectives. After reviewing actual data from the results when asking if satisfied with the overall process; involving pain relief and the arrival time during the survey 15 of 30 agreed which is exactly 50 percent and 11 of 30 were neutral which is 36 percent, therefore 26 of 30 which is 86.6 percent surveyed were not dissatisfied with the new implementation process actually better than the expected 75 percent by 11.6 percent.

Actual results show 13 of 30 surveyed stated that they didn't mind using CIII-V until CII medications arrive and 9 of 30 were neutral which is 22 of 30 resulting in 73.3 percent not minding CIII-V until CII medication arrival. Lastly, noted 25 of 30 surveyed stated that they didn't mind continuing the use of this method over the old process which is 83 percent in favor of the new implementation process.

Survey Questions CIII-V Chi-Square, Percentage Results

STEP	SD	D	N	A	SA
1	42	25	65	62	*76*
2	54	54	54	54	*54*
3	42-54 = -12	25-54 = -29	65-54 = 11	62-54 = 8	*76-54 = 22*
4	(-12X-12) = 144	(-29X-29) = 841	(11X11) = 121	(8X8) = 64	*(22X22) 484*
5	144/54 = 2.6	841/54 = 15.57	121/54 = 2.24	64/54 = 1.19	*484/54 = 8.96*
%	**42/270 = 15.6 %**	**25/270 = 9.3 %**	**65/270 = 24.1 %**	**62/270 = 22.9 %**	**76/270 = 28 %**
6	2.6+15.57+2.24+1.19+8.96 = 30.56 SIGNIFICANCE IN THE FREQUENCY NUMBERS (d.f. = 5-1=4)				

Survey Questions Percentage Results

CIII-CV Questions	SD Strongly Disagree	D Disagree	N Neutral	A Agree	SA Strongly Agree	HIGEHEST %
I was satisfied with the time of my medication	4/30 13.33 %	2/30 6.66 %	12/30 40 %	10/30 33.33%	2/30 6.66 %	A
I was able to provide relief using the alternate medication	0	0	2/30 6.66 %	21/30 70 %	7/30 23.33 %	SA
I do not mind using the medication until original ordered CII arrives	6/30 20 %	2/30 6.66 %	9/30 30 %	5/30 16.66%	8/30 26.66 %	SA
I prefer to have the original CII and no alternate CIII-V medication until its available	1/30 3.33 %	3/30 10 %	6/30 20 %	5/30 16.66%	15/30 50 %	SA
The resident is requesting original CII or creating issues regarding CII ordered	9/30 30 %	3/30 10 %	8/30 26.66%	5/30 16.66%	5/30 16.66 %	SD
CIII-CV took just as long as would have the CII order	15/30 50%	9/30 30 %	3/30 10 %	2/30 6.66 %	1/30 3.33 %	SD
The physician is not okay with receiving the CIII-V in place of CII until available	2/30 6.66 %	5/30 16.66 %	11/30 36.66%	7/30 23.33%	5/30 16.66 %	N
I prefer to continue this process to assure a pain medication for the resident	2/30 6.66 %	0	3/30 10 %	4/30 13.33%	21/30 70 %	SA
I was satisfied with the entire order process	3/30 10 %	1/30 3.33 %	11/30 36.66%	3/30 10 %	12/30 40 %	SA
TOTALS	42/270 15.6 %	25/270 9.3 %	65/270 24.1 %	62/270 22.9 %	76/270 28 %	SA

Conclusion

In conclusion after summarizing the statistical results, it has been proven that the percentages for each given objective totaled higher than necessary for positivity in resolving the system fit error. Chapter seven will discuss conclusions detailing more than statistical data. Recommendations that were or were not made necessary while resolving the system fit error will be given. Possible advancements for future success and or recommendations for further research to keep positive percentages on the rise when dealing with the controlled substance process will also be mentioned if necessary.

Chapter Seven

Conclusions and Recommendations

Introduction

This chapter will interpret, draw conclusions and make recommendations based on the analysis of the results presented in the previous chapter. In short, it details what actions should be taken based upon findings to the system fit error.

Conclusions

Concluding the problematical error, there were two key elements involved. The first element being the dispensing methods of the level II controlled substances to the facilities and clients. Time and sufficient quantity or supply was a major factor. The other key element is the communication process between the physician, LTC's and HHS. The actual time the signed order was received has an impact on the turnaround time; the sooner the pharmacy receives the order, the sooner the order can be processed and shipped to the facilities.

The DEA's overall goal was to eliminate the current dispensing system and have Omnicare Corporations implement a new process for legal purposes that meet the regulations of the CSA. Eliminating all negative outcomes HHS had to devise a time sensitive, cost efficient solution.

The resolution involved restructuring the controlled substance process; and with the proper skill and technique, HHS was able to eliminate this issue while maintaining daily operational tasks. A limitative boundary issue was trying to find a strategic plan that would work around, and eventually fit into the current workflow with the least amount of errors; thus allowing the continuance of production.

Significance of the Project

The importance of this project was that's if all HHS departments involved follow the provided design, implementation and evaluation process as presented, HHS would not only meet the requirements of the DEA, but also eliminate the problematical error altogether. The resolution to the problematical error would demonstrate an exceptional example of a company, HHS amongst other Omnicare organizations being committed to maintaining excellence and integrity within their corporations. As long as all departments involved follow their plan of action accordingly, the resolution and alternative would be an easy fix, even though a lot of detail and thought is required for the actual step by step process.

Data Analysis and Conclusion

The data analysis plan has been created using timed case studies for different controlled substance delivery resolutions and a satisfaction survey that was created to determine the level of satisfaction being received at the facilities. The surveys are illustrated for each objective. The completed surveys determine the accuracy and satisfaction percents of the implemented resolution to the system fit error on a one hundred percent scale involving the controlled substance process.

The conclusions from the studies and surveys conducted indicate that a confirmation is totally in part of the original expectations. In some cases for the actual data the predictions and expectations were substantially higher than expected, which is very positive to the study. Skill and logical reasoning are factors that helped achieve what was to be expected from the objective. The way the alternative was constructed was based on an error so indeed the course of action to fix the error was by compiling data that was a complete opposite.

Objective One Analysis and Conclusion

The first objective analysis design began with objective one involving the controlled substances at a level III-V. This objective states that these level III-V controls will arrive before level II controls when leaving HHS in route to LTC's. This is to determine how long it will take CII medications versus CIII-V medications to reach the pharmacy. Objective one entailed controlled substances at a level III-V taking just as long as level II controls when leaving HHS in route to LTC's. This was also to determine the length of time.

A ninety-five percent acceptability rate on turnaround time was a factor due to the level III-V medications having lower processing standards compared to level II medications. This process was to help relieve pain by at least fifty percent. A ninety-five percent acceptability rate on turnaround time was the expected factor for CIII-V medications. The new implantation process is twenty percent better in terms of delivery over the old process.

The new implementation process was to help relieve pain by at least fifty percent and should provide customer satisfaction of at least seventy percent as well although customer satisfaction will be mentioned in depth in objective three. The actual surveyed percentage results were ninety-three percent. Objective one was a total success on all aspects of time and satisfaction.

Objective Two Analysis and Conclusion

Objective two involved a prescription order type (also known as a RX order type) will take just as long as RXP order types to process. This is to determine how long the entire process will take from start to finish. Objective one will also determine whether or not an RX order type will arrive before a RXP order type when leaving HHS going to LTC's. Objective two consisted of the order entry process changing from one order type for medication entry to another order type to decrease the turnaround times of delivery. HHS will be eliminating the RXP profile only order type to enter level II-V medications and in its place a RX order type will be the only use for order entry for any and all level II-V medications. This is to decrease the turnaround time from HHS to the facilities by at least fifty percent. The expected increase will be at least eighty-five percent satisfaction for timely arrival of the medication from the pharmacy to the facilities.

Actual results show that the new implementation process is twenty percent greater in terms of delivery over the old process using CIII-V medications instead. This is less than five percent from one hundred percent and an eleven percent advantage over the projected outcome.

In addition to the current study findings, seventy-five percent satisfaction rate was necessary for delivery time as well. The data results showed eighty percent satisfaction on delivery, forty percent each going to agreeing and neutrality. This also coincides with the previous percent delivery rate of CIII-V medications in one to five hours. Objective two was a total success on all aspects of time and satisfaction.

Objective Three Analysis and Conclusion

Objective three involved positive results of more satisfied than discontented LTC's if they receive CIII-V medications in place of CII medications until the CII's are available for shipment. This objective consisted of whether or not facilities are angered by receiving CIII-CV medications in place of CII's until arrival from HHS to LTC's. This objective also consists of whether or not facilities are angered by receiving CIII-CV medications in place of CII's until arrival from HHS to LTC's. This objective involved pain relief satisfaction and overall arrival time satisfaction as well all due to the fact that objective three is about customer satisfaction.

When involving customer satisfaction, an overall satisfaction rate needed to be at least seventy-five percent leaving twenty-five percent for errors. The arrival times should still have a percent of ninety-five for satisfaction for CIII-V medications and a fifty percent satisfaction for pain relief from the previous objectives. After reviewing actual data from the previous results when asking if satisfied with the overall process; pain relief and the arrival time, there were less than fifteen percent surveyed that were dissatisfied with the new implementation process when involving arrival time and pain relief. Objective three was a total success on all aspects of pain relief and arrival times.

These findings and resolutions to the system fit error are long term and can be used not only within HHS but also with all other branches that use similar processing and delivery methods.

Policy Recommendations

Making formal recommendations regarding a preferred alternative is not applicable with this situation. HHS and many other pharmacies were taking major financial losses due to the system fit error. This was a major aspect being that it involved all controlled substances. The controlled substances are of top priority and the major aspect within the company that brings in its revenue. If an accurate, positive and satisfactory supply of narcotics cannot be distributed to the facilities that HHS services, they would in turn be forced to withdraw contracts and the LTC's would then take on other vendors who could meet their supply needs and satisfaction demands.

As far as alternative options such as filing bankruptcy, combining some of the smaller branches for joint ventures or trying to eliminate employee benefits to accommodate for the fees issued from the DEA are not actually alternatives. These would be actions to take if all else failed being that the results of these outcomes involves downsizing or cutting cost by employee elimination of some sort. Either way it would be a bad reflection on the pharmacy in the eyes of society since all of the alternatives leave the employees without a say in anything.

In the healthcare field it is major that the code of ethics and morality remain first and foremost, this is because it is involving the servicing of all people, from infants to the elderly. Everyone depends on pharmacies and without them there would be no medication distribution. Instead of alternatives, it was a better plan of action to entirely fix the system fit error, thus showing integrity for the field of pharmacy as a whole entity.

The recommendations and alternative for the system fit error will have a major impact on the pharmacy policy in a positive aspect. It will also affect future programs or policies because now HHS has an established plan of action in place that abides by the requirements of the DEA, FDA and the CSA. The alternative to the system fit error will be continued as it is already in place and working successfully within the pharmacy.

Even with talks of requiring signatures for all medications controls and non-controls as mentioned in the plan limitations, the alternative that has been initiated can be altered and will uphold if necessary because the same case study can be revamped and implemented accordingly while keeping the flow of current production.

Recommendations for Further Research

There are a few plan limitations that could require further research. The data may have resulted differently if the study was done on first or second shift as compared to third. Situations could arise if the data results begin to skew negatively in the beginning which would mean no positive results or very limited positive results.

Recommending further research that involves the elimination of processing controlled substances altogether, and possibly replacing them with a high demand item such as non narcotic intravenous and chemotherapy medications would be good to research. This would also eliminate the system fit error, and if revenue can be replaced HHS would not suffer a loss. Other things to consider would be researching many costs saving ideas and acting on one of the top three alternatives that would create the least harm to the company as a whole.

It can also be recommended that research be done to discuss how serious the DEA is about requiring signatures for all controlled substances. Even though adjustments can be made to accommodate, it is still beneficial to have a superior hand and a leading start on the errors and dilemmas, allowing more time for resolutions and alternatives.

Summary

The DEA's overall goal was to eliminate the current dispensing system and have Omnicare Corporations implement a new process for legal purposes that meet the regulations of the CSA, which has in fact been done and implemented. The implemented plan was to avoid losing any of the branches or to eliminate possible HHS mergers. There are no longer talks of branch closings, nor mergers, which is highly positive in today's society.

The plan was to be a time sensitive solution to halt fines and eliminate revenue loss overall. This plan has been implemented during operational hours, abiding by the allotted time given from the DEA. All fines have been ceased and all lost revenue has been recovered due to the pharmacy being able to continue to process pharmaceutical orders while devising the plan and putting the plan in motion

The resolution to the system fit error restructured the controlled substance process; using proper skill and technique, managing to maintain the current workflow with the least amount of errors; thus continuing the current production flow as well. The importance of this project not only met the requirements of the DEA, but first and foremost eliminated the problematical error altogether. The resolution to the problematical error has indeed demonstrated an exceptional example of excellence and integrity within HHS amongst other Omnicare organizations now using this new implemented alternative method of order processing.

Lastly, concluding my project thesis will be a reflection looking back on the start of the project to the current state of the resolved system fit error; the completed project thesis.

Appendix A

Reflections

This appendix is a discussion of my personal thoughts reflected through my project thesis. It indirectly reflects my present thought process through my educational trials and tribulations nearing the completion of the Spring Arbor University Management and Organizational Development program. It also analyzes and summarizes my feelings, learning outcomes and my mental state of self-being from initiation of the project thesis to the conclusion of the MOD program.

My reflection commonly describes my conceptualization and concrete beliefs as a student as well as a soon to be graduate. This project thesis has questions within itself such as; what generalized learning can be used for researchers and or other research situations, expected and unexpected outcomes and what design and intellectual techniques I used during my research analysis. This appendix will conclude my thesis project by detailing my overall career learning's. A concluding summary of my reflections, also known as my experiences with this project thesis as well as my college experience in the MOD program in direct relations to my current employer, my personal and social activities as well as my life in broad-spectrum; all similarities and differences will be noted.

My personal thoughts about my project thesis are minimal. I do believe that this project thesis has helped develop, maintain and critique my writing technique and style overall. This project has improved my thinking ability and it has made me develop more as an individual within my personal as well as my professional life. On the other hand my thesis project has indirectly reassured many of my world views. It has shown me that there are still individuals out there in the workforce whom believe that after a lot of hard work and effort it is okay to treat others unfair, even in today's society when there are so many advancements taking place in the world.

When I began my project thesis it started out as something I could fix within my place of employment. I did not choose this topic of controlled substances because I was seeking a topic for my project thesis, I chose this because I actually have a passion in the field of pharmacy and I cared enough about my company despite their unethical ways, to make a positive change overall that would benefit all employees. I also wanted to create an alternative to benefit the patients that we as pharmaceutical provider serve. Medicine is for the ill, and I felt and still remain within the same ramification that ill individuals should not have to suffer from the stupidity that is evolving in everyday society.

I can honestly state that at the end of the implementation of my idea that benefited the pharmacy greatly, I didn't foresee the promotion of someone with less skill and knowledge surpassing me without any input or feedback on my behalf. As an effect of that, I am assuming my employer didn't see the pending lawsuit that I filed in their future of the pharmacy either.

From a student point of view, I am very proud of having accomplished a project thesis. When I began this program a year ago, I used to think that the ten page critical synthesis papers were lengthy. Now I can write a ten page paper in no time, with no problems or complaints. I have grown so much as a writer and I also realized that being in the MOD program; management and business is the field I prefer over pharmaceuticals. I enjoy the management setting and all that comes along with it. I enjoy writing and improving my skills, techniques and style. I try to take specific feedback from my graded papers and reuse the techniques to perfect my writing. I have noted that where I used to get satisfactory grades on my critical synthesis papers, I now get full credit and fewer comments. Just being able to notice a difference in my own writing and the grading of my assignments shows that my learning abilities and cognitive skills have advanced as well. Learning in my opinion is so powerful in today's society. It is a tool that can be used as input and output interchangeably.

Being that the project thesis was started over a year ago; the hardest part in completing a project like this is staying on task. When we as a cohort came down to the final two weeks of class it was very troubling listening to my fellow classmates state that they were behind or they were not going to be finished at the same time as myself. I have empathy for them but at the same time, it is the MOD program. The title of the program; organizational development speaks for itself. I recall repeatedly on numerous occasions various instructors stating *"Do not fall behind"*.

Our instructors made it very clear that staying on task is detrimental to this project thesis and once behind it would be difficult to regain a current state physically and mentally. I myself chose to listen. Despite any and all problems in my life I always put forth some effort and managed to turn in some type of completed chapter on the due date. I am assuming this is not one of those *"I told you so"* moments; this is a moment of truth for a lot of individuals in my class. I do hope and pray that we all walk together on graduation day.

My project thesis evolved from countless hours of time and effort. This project thesis has questions within itself such as; what generalized learning can be used for researchers and or other research situations, expected and unexpected outcomes and what design and intellectual techniques I used during my research analysis. As far as researchers and other research situations my alternative resolution has not only been implemented at my pharmacy but it is being utilized at other pharmacies as well. The general design was set up on a win-win basis. It was to generally be cost efficient and time effective. It was geared toward many positives and minimal negatives.

When concerning other researchers or situations, I would actually suggest utilizing this same design if and when the DEA decides to require signatures on all controlled substances and possibly all medications in general. The easiest way to see results is to conduct surveys and do a compare and contrast study using the process of elimination to narrow down the best method of use depending on what is required of the DEA, FDA and or the CSA. I myself like research, so I feel that the more surveys conducted the better the outcomes. Feedback of any kind is always useful.

On the other hand I would give a suggestion to future researchers; even though third shift is quieter in regards to getting task completed, it would be possibly more beneficial if the study could be conducted with the input of first and third shift. It leaves more people to be involved to divide the workload. A possible burn out risk is a factor when conducting a study on third shift being that there is minimal staff on third shift, employees are typically struggling to stay awake, and a lot of necessary contacts may not be available. Any or all of these factors could bias the results, and that makes for a null study, which is useless.

A positive aspect of conducting studies on third shift is that the employees are more relaxed. This is typically because they deal with less drama involved with management. In the pharmacy, we as employees and a team were able to listen to music while calculating data. For some individuals the soothing sounds of music are relaxing and help to relieve or ease stress. When trying to implement a major alternative that can impact the future of the pharmacy it is necessary to remain stress free. Limit the dictatorship and work as a team. Making everyone feel like their input is necessary and all opinions are valued makes the entire research process conduct more professionally, precisely, flawless and without argumentative behaviors. These are just a few of the techniques I used during my project thesis; alternative solution to the system fit error at Heartland Healthcare Services.

Describing my conceptualization and concrete beliefs as a student as well as a soon to be graduate; I feel so accomplished at this moment in my life. I am a believer that when one door shuts another door opens. I did indeed have to face an ethical dilemma during the course of the MOD program, but at the same time while one of my employers shunned me, my other employer promoted me. I was a first beginning to doubt myself as an employee, trying to find faults within myself of any sort to relate to my unfair treatment. I then asked my other employer who told me, it wasn't me; I give one hundred percent if not more with all duties assigned to me. My supervisor reassured me that it was indeed them and they deserve what the outcomes of my lawsuit holds. I had to recapture my mind frame and remind myself that I am an overachiever; I put forth my best efforts with any and everything I do, regardless of how tedious the task may be. Based upon this ethical dilemma I will never let anyone make me doubt my sound judgment of self worth ever again.

My current abilities in MOD reside with my higher power and SAU for helping develop my skills. I am graduating from the MOD program with a positive outlook that I have indeed learned multiple key aspects from this program and I have utilized a lot of them professionally and personally. I did decide to continue my education and begin Graduate school in the fall, and work on my Masters until I gain my Doctorate. When I entered into the business field, I knew in my heart this is where I belonged. From all the promotions from lead technician to supervisor, I knew I should stay within management and make this a career goal with endless possibilities and opportunities.

Now as an effect of finding what I like to do in life, I want to give back my knowledge and teach at a university as well. I too would like to instruct students and tell them that life is what they make of it. I want students to know that college is very necessary for any type of progression because skill enhancement is necessary regardless of the time or setting.

I believe that I have touched on all aspects required of this reflection. Now I would like to use the remainder of my appendix to touch base on a few aspects of my personal life reflecting upon my studies at SAU in the MOD program. I am indeed a little bothered by the fact that we as a cohort have come this far and we are just now finding out that some individuals will not be finish May 25, 2010. The last few sessions of our time together as a cohort, I came to find out that there were many individuals whom felt as if we were not a close knit group. They felt as if the entire experience was not a positive or fulfilling experience. If I may be as bold as to say with all due respect the nerve of some individuals, to speak such madness is outright unacceptable. I cannot believe that people actually fixed their mouths to speak such things to individuals whom have been with one another for at least a year, in a Christian university and within the same cohort every Tuesday. It felt as if with those words being said some individuals learned nothing from the MOD program.

We were a cohort with many faces. We shared very detailed information with one another and by stating that you felt the experience was unpleasant, a waste of time, useless or even to give poor evaluations to instructors based upon the negligence on the students' performance just shows selfishness of one's self. I can recall countless arguments with no meaning or morale, unnecessary bickering, judgments being placed upon one another and even segregation of various types. I too had my faults in class but never once did I ever try to make another individual feel as if their presence was making my life learning experience miserable. Again, SAU being a Christian university I expected better. Age had nothing to do with the various attitudes in class. This made me wonder what my classmates were like outside of class and at work if this is what was taking place in a Christian university. I give all due credit to the instructors, with all belief in my higher power, I too hope to be a member of the SAU faculty. The instructors deal with so much, and being able to hold a professional composure is phenomenal in my eyesight when dealing with various personality types.

As I near the end of my reflections I can honestly say that it has been a very interesting journey. I have graduated from college three times previously and this by far is my most memorable completion of a program. There were many first time experiences for myself and preparing for the Master's program I am sure there will be many more.

SAU was the first college where I had ever felt empathy toward other student's situations, ethical dilemmas and life's trials and tribulations in general. SAU was the first college where I ever disclosed close and personal facts and information with a cohort as a group or with individual students. SAU is the first college where I have given my last anything to help a fellow classmate. SAU is the first college where we eat and pray together as a family. SAU is the first college where I conducted a group assignment in class through the communicational lines of face book. SAU is the first college where I gained motivation from face book. SAU is the first college for prayers to specifically go out to my fellow classmates; for completion of all their assignments and necessary requirements for November 2010's ceremony. SAU is the first college I attended that I actually enjoyed writing a project thesis. Lastly, SAU is the first college where I maintained a SAU GPA of 3.9.

In conclusion, from starting with *Adult development and Life Planning* and ending with *Values; Personal and Social* in attendance at SAU, the one thing I am graduating with is the respect of oneself and the respect of others. Congratulations to all SAU graduates including myself and good luck to all students, staff and faculty with any aspect of life's journey. I pray that our higher power be with all SAU beings including family and friends before and after graduation.

Definition of Terms

Term	Definition
AIDS	Acquired Immune Deficiency Syndrome or Acquired Immunodeficiency Syndrome
ASCP	American Society for Consultant Pharmacists Organization
ASHP	American Society of Health-Systems Pharmacists Organization
CEO	Chief Executive Officer; The highest-ranking executive in a company or organization, responsible for carrying out policies for the board of directors
CSA	Controlled Substance Act of 1970; implementing legislation for narcotic drugs
C2	Controlled Substances Level II
DEA	Drug Enforcement Agency; lead agency for domestic enforcement of the drug policy of the US
FDA	Food and Drug Administration; United States Department of Health and Human Services

HHS	Heartland Healthcare Services; Pharmaceutical Company.
HMO	Health Maintenance Organization
INCB	International Narcotics Control Board
IV Dept.	Intravenous Dept; processes all intravenous medications
JCAHO	Joint Commission on Accreditation of Health Care Organization
LTC/SLF/ALF	Long Term Care, Supported Living & Assisted Living Facilities; nursing facilities for which HHS provides service
NR	No Refill
NRX	Non-Authorized Prescription Order type for medication entry stating that the medication needs prior authorization. Typically CII-V's
PF	Profile Only The medication will not be sent to the facility, only profiled for medical record purposes

PV1	Prescription Verification Stage One
RXP	Refill Profile The first time the prescription is received it will not be sent just profiled only and will be sent on demand from the facility at a later date
THC	Tetrahydrocannabinol (Also known as Dronabinol)
TIC	Tickle File
USP	United States Pharmacopeia

www.ingramcontent.com/pod-product-compliance
Lightning Source LLC
Chambersburg PA
CBHW050741180526
45159CB00003B/1308